Tango Zen: Walking Dance Meditation

D1293376

Tango Zen:

Walking Dance Meditation

— Chan Park

Tango Zen House 2004

For more information, contact:

Tango Zen House

http://www.TangoZen.com

TangoZen@hotmail.com

To my teacher Shunryu Suzuki and

my Tango partner and wife Eugenia Park. . .

Contents

Introduction

Would you like to meditate while dancing Tango? Yes, Buddha can teach you to dance Tango through Zen. You might ask, "How does Tango have anything to do with Zen?"

Tango Zen is an innovative yet natural way of meditating while dancing Tango. Referring to striking similarities between the two, this book will introduce methods through which Tango dancers and non-dancers can practice Tango Zen to experience and enjoy the wonderful benefits, which both Tango and Zen have to offer.

Everybody knows meditation is a good thing. For example, Zen meditation, if practiced properly, can create balance, calmness, groundedness, centering, and harmony in mind and body.

However, it is difficult to meditate for many reasons. Meditation is mainly practiced while sitting with legs crossed to support and ground one's body. Unfortunately this sitting posture can create uncomfortable feelings and even pains before you benefit from the meditation practice. In addition, despite the importance of practicing meditation regularly, it can be difficult to stick to it with regularity due to the hectic life style we live everyday.

Can one meditate while moving around instead of sitting down? Although it appears to be sedate and passive, Zen meditation can also be practiced in more active ways than the sitting posture. For example, walking meditation has been practiced among Buddhists since the Buddha himself practiced it. Other forms of Zen meditation in motion can also be found in sports and performing arts.

Tango is a walking dance—a special gift from Argentina to the world. Unlike Tango images of sexy and provocative movements commonly featured in media, Tango is a social dance that should be danced while walking. Of course, one embraces the partner and listens to music while walking. Benefits of Tango dancing can be explained in many aspects including social, physical, and emotional; however, the effects and benefits of meditation are experienced and shared among avid Tango dancers.

The main goal of meditation is to discover and reconcile one's own nature. To reach that goal, Zen teaches us to devote 100% of our attention to what we are doing Here Now. Tango is a dance of connection, uniting one and one's partner while walking and listening to music—together. Tango can be fully enjoyed only if one completely surrenders to and connects with one's partner, both physically and emotionally, while dancing. Therefore, once recognizing similarities and benefits of the two, one can truly unite and practice Tango and Zen. One can meditate while dancing Tango, experiencing deeper appreciation of physical, emotional, and even spiritual aspects of inner-self. That is, one can practice Tango Zen: Walking Dance Meditation.

Tango, Tango, Tango. . .

—*Chan Park*

Tango Zen: Walking Dance Meditation

What is Tango?

Tango is a social dance originated from the streets and salons of Buenos Aires, Argentina. Specifically, Tango is traced back to African music and dance, which were brought to Argentina by black slaves from Africa. Early twentieth century, European immigrants, mainly Italians, Spaniards, French and Germans, influenced the styles of Tango, to which we are accustomed.

Unlike other social dances, danced by a couple, Tango is characterized as a dance of improvisation based on mutual communication between two partners moving as one. It also involves a great deal of concentration, creativity, and precision of each dancer.

What is Zen?

Zen is a Buddhist meditation technique designed to free one's mind from slavery to reason and logic. The purpose of Zen practice is to realize and to express one's true nature through meditation, ultimately attaining *Satori*, the Zen moment, that is, the indescribable state of mind—Enlightenment. Zen practice, when reconciled with one's everyday life, creates balance, calmness, groundedness, centering, and harmony in mind and body.

What is Tango Zen?

Zen meditation can be practiced in forms other than the sitting posture of zazen. For example, walking meditation has been practiced among Buddhists since the Buddha himself practiced it upon Enlightenment. Other forms of Zen meditation in motion can also be found in sports and performing arts.

Tango Zen combines Zen meditation principles with Tango dancing. Tango Zen is meditation in motion, and, if practiced properly, may enable Tango dancers and non-dancers alike to meditate and experience Zen moment while dancing Tango.

How to practice Tango Zen

Although it is almost impossible to completely describe the Zen moment in words, there are some exercises that can help interested Tango dancers meditate and align mind and body with a path towards the Zen moment.

To meditate while dancing Tango, one may practice the following ideas adapted from Zen:

— *The Right Posture, The Right State of Mind*
— *Dance Here Now*
— *Letting Go*
— *Releasing The Ego*
— *Expressing Our Own Nature—Buddha Nature*
— *Two Bodies, Four Legs, and One Heart*
— *Music: The Heart of Tango*
— *Practice, Practice, Practice*
— *Confidence: Absence of Self-Consciousness*
— *Experience, Not Philosophy*
— *Beginner's Mind*
— *Tango, Zen, Enlightenment… Everyday Life*

The Right Posture, The Right State of Mind

In Zen, taking the right posture is itself, having the right state of mind. In this state, body, breath, and mind come together as one reality when we meditate. As in Zen, in order to have the right posture while dancing Tango, it is important to keep the spine straight and still, chin tucked in, the top of head pushed up towards the ceiling, diaphragm pushed down towards lower abdomen, and the whole body relaxed at the same time.

When our posture is right, we automatically breathe correctly. Breathing should be natural and constant. For deep breathing, focus must be placed upon *Dan Tien*, the center of energy below the navel, instead of chest.

Do not lose your knowledge that man's proper estate is an upright posture, an intransigent mind, and a step that travels unlimited roads.
— *Ayn Rand*

The state of mind that exists when you sit in the right posture is, itself, enlightenment.   —Shunryu Suzuki

The body is a sacred garment.   —Martha Graham

There is only the one Way—straight, open, and utterly empty of obstructions.   —Yuan-Wu

The three main things in zazen [sitting meditation posture] are posture, breathing, and attitude of mind—and correctly practiced, they lead to the very principle of zazen: hishiryo *consciousness, thinking without thinking.*   —Taisen Deshimaru

What we call "I" is just a swinging door which moves when we inhale and when we exhale.   —Shunryu Suzuki

The dancer's body is simply the luminous manifestation of the soul.
                —Isadora Duncan

To keep the body in good health is a duty...otherwise we shall not be able to keep our mind strong and clear. —Buddha

Technique—bodily control—must be mastered only because the body must not stand in the way of the soul's expression. —La Meri

Sitting quietly, doing nothing, spring comes, and the grass grows by itself. —Zen Proverb

Dance Here Now

While dancing Tango, one should be mindful of each movement of one's own and partner's, moment by moment, with total concentration. Zen teaches us to do everything with total presence of mind. We need to concentrate on what we are doing now. Forget about the past and leave the future alone. While dancing Tango, we don't have to go anywhere or achieve anything. Simply Dance Here Now, with total concentration on each movement.

Be Here Now. —Baba Ram Das

Tango at its best is about being 100% in the present, completely aware, totally focused on my partner and the music. It's about being relaxed and non-judgmental: not attached to the future (anticipating) or the past (obsessing about the mistake I made 10 steps ago). —Kate Withey

When you do something, you should burn yourself completely, like a good bonfire, leaving no trace of yourself. —Shunryu Suzuki

Zen thrives on paradox. The more you think about it, the less you will really understand. The more you try to seek Enlightenment, the further you will get from it.
                    —From "Zen in 10 Simple Lesson" by A.M. Lee and D. Weiss

I have no desire to prove anything by dancing. I have never used it as an outlet or a means of expressing myself. I just dance. I just put my feet in the air and move them around. —Fred Astaire

We look backward too much and we look forward too much; thus we miss the only eternity of which we can be absolute sure-eternal present, for it is always now. —William Phelps

Dance as if no one were watching, Sing as if no one were listening, And live every day as if it were your last. —Anonymous

Move now and the way will open.   —Anonymous (Zen Proverb)

If you walk, just walk.
If you sit, just sit.
But don't wobble.
                    —*Yunmen*

No valid plans for the future can be made by those who have no capacity for living now.   —*Alan Watts*

Time is not a line, but a series of now-points.   —*Taisen Deshimaru*

Letting Go

Whatever feelings and thoughts arise while dancing Tango—just let them pass with no attachment to anything. Zen teaches us to open our minds and see things as they are. Be ready to let feelings and thoughts come and go without engaging them. Resist the impulse of analyzing or judging them. However, don't push away or avoid them either. Just listen to the music and dance.

The less you expect, the less you judge, the less you cling to this or that experience as significant, the further you will progress. —Ram Das

Whatever there is attachment
Associate with it
Brings endless misery.
                              —Gampopa

Inside yourself or outside, you never have to change what you see, only the way you see it. —Thaddeus Golas

The only way to make sense out of change is to plunge into it, move with it, and join the dance. —Alan W. Watts

Dance first. Think later. It's the natural order. —Samuel Beckett

When I dance, I cannot judge, I cannot hate, I cannot separate myself from life. I can only be joyful and whole, that is why I dance.
—Hans Bos

Never criticize your dance partner. —Brave Combo

Sitting quietly, doing nothing, spring comes, and the grass grows by itself. —Zen saying

To understand everything is to forgive everything.   —Buddha

The greatest obstacles to inner peace are disturbing emotions such as anger, attachment, fear and suspicion, while love and compassion and a sense of universal responsibility are the sources of peace and happiness.   —Dalai Lama

Your problem is you're... too busy holding onto your unworthiness.
—Ram Dass

Belief means not wanting to know what is true.
—Friedrich Nietzsche

Releasing The Ego

While dancing Tango, we must release our ego. Zen teaches us to sever our identification with the ego, which makes us believe and anticipate what and how things, the next steps or figures, for example, ought to be. Once we release the ego, we can move with flow of energy, moment by moment.

The magical leader's first concern is the couple, not the steps he wants to lead. For this to happen, the magical leader must surrender to his partner in the same way as the follower must surrender to his lead. He must surrender any image of what he wants/expects to do and open himself to the possibility of what might develop.
—Johanna Siegmann from Tango-L

Dancing: The Highest Intelligence in the Freest Body. —Isadora Duncan

A woman must be completely centered and balanced so she can be able to move at an instant's notice in any direction.

She must be in complete control of her body in order to surrender control of where she is going.

She needs to be completely grounded so she can be free enough to feel that she is flying.

Her body must be toned enough to provide enough resistance to the man to respond to his proposed changes of direction in a completely relaxed way that avoids obstruction.

The woman must be mentally alert in order to keep her mind empty in the present time in order to respond at the speed and with the precision that it is required. —Sally Potter's Tango Aphorisms

And nobody knows how fearful is the opposite sex to one's own. I realized that if I cannot surrender in Tango, I cannot dance. To dance I have to surrender. —Susana Miller

The magical leader's first concern is the couple, not the steps he wants to lead. For this to happen, the magical leader must surrender to his partner in the same way as the follower must surrender to his lead. He must surrender any image of what he wants/expects to do and open himself to the possibility of what might develop.
—Johanna Siegmann from Tango-L

Flow with whatever may happen and let your mind be free: Stay centered by accepting whatever you are doing. This is the ultimate.
—Zhuangzi

Expressing Our Own Nature—Buddha Nature

We dance Tango to express our own true nature, not attempting to accomplish anything special. The purpose of Zen practice is to express our own nature— the Self or our own Buddha nature, without any desire to accomplish something. When we dance Tango, we should express our true nature, feeling free from any goal or desire, which causes the suffering in life, according to the Buddhism.

When you become you, Zen becomes Zen. —Shunryu Suzuki

To dance, above all, is to enter into the motions of life. It is an action, a movement, a process. The dance of life is not so much a metaphor as a fact; to dance is to know oneself alone and to celebrate it
—Sherman Paul

The truest expression of a people is in its dance and in its music. Bodies never lie.   —Agnes de Mille

Dancing is the last word in life. In dancing one draws nearer to oneself.
—Jean Dubuffet

A good artist will come out and show you his specialties and tell you who he is, and that's about it.   —Joan Acocella

Dance is an art that imprints on the soul. It is with you every moment, it expresses itself in everything you do.   —Shirley Maclaine

Learning to walk sets you free. Learning to dance gives you the greatest freedom of all: to express your whole self, the person you are.
—Melissa Hayden

Tango lets us express anger...,love..., passion..., in a socially accepted way.
—Leandro Paulou

I see dance being used as communication between body and soul, to express what it too deep to find for words. —Ruth St. Denis

You make it [flamenco] modern by revealing yourself, not with embellishments. What is difficult is revealing yourself. —Eva Yerbabuena

The Dancer believes that his art has something to say which cannot be expressed in words or in any other way than by dancing. There are times when the simple dignity of movement can fulfill the function of a volume of words. —Doris Humphrey

Dance is your pulse, your heartbeat, your breathing. It's the rhythm of your life. It's the expression in time and movement, in happiness, joy, sadness and envy. —Jaques D'ambroise

Two Bodies, Four Legs, and One Heart

When two partners embrace to dance Tango, the connection has to be established and sustained throughout the dance. Zen invites us to experience Oneness by transcending all the differences separating two opposite sides. In Tango, we should have no room for Separateness, which is opposite to Oneness. Between partners, when we embrace and dance, we must strive to become One, dancing along in the Universe in harmony.

Good is bad and bad is good. —Zen saying

Dancing's just a conversation between two people. Talk to me.
—Hope Floats

Dance is communication, and so the great challenge is to speak clearly, beautifully, and with inevitability. —Martha Graham

Zen can be defined as the unity of man and the universe, as the rhythm of the mind with changing forms, as a state of One-ness in which all distinction of I and not-I knower and known, seer and seen, are set aside.   —Alan Watts

Enlightenment is like the reflection of the moon in the water. The moon does not get wet and the water is not separated.   —Hashida

The One and the All. Mingle and move
Without discriminating. Live in this awareness
and you'll stop worrying about not being perfect.   —Seng-T'san

Do not follow the ideas of others, but learn to listen to the voice within yourself. Your body and mind will become clear and you will realize the unity of all things.   —Dogen

The essence of the beautiful is unity in variety.
—William Somerset Maugham

In the embrace, being there in body and soul with another, holding yet letting go, each knows a freedom.
—Alan Kremen from ReporTANGO

Dancing with the feet is one thing, but dancing with the heart is another.   —Anonymous

Relativity teaches us the connection between the different descriptions of one and the same reality.   —Albert Einstein

Build for your team a feeling of oneness, of dependence on one another and of strength to be derived by unity.   —Vince Lombardi

Music: The Heart of Tango

As air is life to our body, music is a driving force in the mind while dancing Tango. Music is heard in the present moment, a tangible reminder of our present yet impermanent existence amid the continuum of time and space. It reminds us to *Be Here Now* while dancing Tango. It is known that Buddhists use *mantras*, the chanting or the repetition of a word or phrase as a tool to maintain concentration and awareness. Through music, our mind and body can be harmonized so that there is no separation between them while dancing. For the purpose meditation, we can select songs that are simple and rhythmic so as to keep the mind from wandering off while we dance.

The party is done on a Tango that has definite beat, because people's hearts beat at that rhythm. . . Outside of the beat, there is no party!
—Susana Miller

A milonguero is a slave of the music, the tempo and the space. When he dances, music invades his body and is translated into his steps and movements. He never misses a tempo. Such blending with the music is what produces a sensation that their bodies are actually speaking.
—Cacho Dante

Dancing can reveal all the mystery that music conceals.
—Charles Baudelaire

A child sings before it speaks, dances almost before it walks, music is with us from the beginning. —Pamela Brown

Even the ears must dance. —Natalia Makarova

And those who were seen dancing were thought to be insane by those who could not hear the music. —Friedrich Wilhelm Nietzsche

Music begins to atrophy when it departs too far from the dance.
—Ezra Pound

Let yourself be filled with the music to be able to interpret it.
—Guillermina Quiroga

The Tango is a special form of communication with your partner and expressing yourself in relation to the music.   —Jessica Bijvoet

Boy, you have to honor the music more than your mother.
—Omar Vega's old teacher

Practice, Practice, Practice

In order to reach total concentration and free the mind while dancing Tango, we should maintain the spirit of repetition. All Zen activities provide us with an approach to perfection with total attention to minute details. Only through the repetition of preset movements can we reach perfection, allowing the body to take over to free the mind from concentration. Thus, when we practice or dance Tango, it is OK to repeat the same basic steps over and over again.

What we hope ever to do with ease, we must first learn to do with diligence. —Samuel Johnson

Often the only thing standing between a man and his dreams is the will to do what is necessary and the faith to believe it is possible.
—R. DeVos

Do not be carried away by anything outward or conventional. Zen must be seized with bare hands, with no gloves on. —D. T. Suzuki

In life as in dance: Grace glides on blistered feet. —Alice Abrams

Make the impossible possible, the possible easy and the easy elegant. —Moshe Feldenkreis

Master technique and then forget about it and be natural.
—Anna Pavlova

Great works are performed not by strength buy by perseverance.
—Samuel Johnson

Practice means to perform, over and over again in the face of all obstacles, some act of vision, of faith, of desire. Practice is a means of inviting the perfection desired. —Martha Graham

Try again. Fail again. Fail better.   —Samuel Beckett

A jug fills drop by drop.   —Buddha

Diligence overcomes difficulties, sloth makes them.
*   —Benjamin Franklin*

Learning is not attained by chance, it must be sought for with ardor
and diligence.   —Abigail Adams

No victor believes in chance.   —Friedrich Nietzsche

Confidence: Absence of Self-Consciousness

For Tango to be Tango, we need to make each and every movement with confidence. No hesitation. In Zen we strive to celebrate our own nature, our unique gifts and abilities. We are who we are and, likewise, we dance Tango the way we are. For self-confidence, we need to block our self-consciousness by stopping the self-critical monologue, e.g. the mental chatter while dancing Tango. Be easy on yourself, as you are the best you can be Here and Now!

The point we emphasize is strong confidence in our original nature.
—Shunryu Suzuki

He who hesitates is lost.   —English proverb

He is able who thinks he is able.   —Buddha

No on can make you feel inferior without your consent.
—Eleanor Roosevelt

I am what I am and that's all that I am. *—Popeye*

Whether you think you can or you can't-you are right. *—Henry Ford*

Your love for yourself is only shown when you are dancing freely.
—Anonymous

First we have to believe, and then we believe. *—Martha Graham*

All you need in this life is ignorance and confidence; then success is sure.
—Mark Twain

Skill and confidence are an unconquered army. *—George Herbert*

To succeed in life, you need two things: ignorance and confidence.
                                                        —Mark Twain

Confidence is contagious; so is lack of confidence.   *—Vince Lombardi*

Experience tells you what to do; confidence allows you to do it.
                                                        —Stan Smith

Confidence is preparation. Everything else is beyond your control.
                                                        —Richard Kline

Experience, Not Philosophy

The pure form of Tango is the dancing of two partners. Any intellectual or philosophical discussions as to what Tango really is may run a risk of getting entangled with dualistic ideas. Like Zen, Tango can be beyond what words can express. It can open a door only to the one willing to experience pure and delicate joy in its pure form. In Tango, like all other practices, to taste essence one must do; that is, one must dance. So drop your pen. Turn off your computer. Go out dancing Tango.

The Tango can debated, and we have debated over it, but it still guards, as does all that is truthful, a secret. —Jorge Luis Borges

One who knows does not say, one who says does not know.
—Zen saying

I tried and it worked. I want you to try it for yourself. —Buddha

Dance isn't something that can be explained in words; it has to be danced. —Paige Arden

No, I can't explain the dance to you; if I could say it—I wouldn't have to dance it! —Isadora Duncan

Is there anyone so wise as to learn by the experience of others?
—Voltaire

A dog is not considered a good dog because he is a good barker. A man is not considered a good man because he is a good talker. —Buddha

Shall I compare this life to a lightning flash or a drop of dew? Before I have even spoken these words, it has passed. —Sengai

Good dancers have mostly better heels than heads. —Thomas Fuller

Talk about dance? Dance is not something to talk about. Dance is to dance.   —Peter Saint James

Tango-L stands for Tango-Lost and Tango-A Tango-Anarchy.
                                                        —Anonymous

What one has not experienced, one will never understand in print.
                                                        —Isadora Duncan

Those who can't dance say the music is no good.
                                        —Anonymous (Jamaican Proverb)

A good education is usually harmful to a dancer. A good calf is better than a good head.   —Agnes De Mille

Beginner's Mind

When we embrace and do *salida*, Tango opens a door of infinite possibilities as long as our mind is ready for new experiences and wisdom. Zen teaches us to deal with the world with a humble, *I-don't-know mind*, a beginner's mind. With a beginner's mind, what matters is a willingness to adapt to and to learn from the present situation, not insisting on prior experience or mediocrity. For each movement we make, we must be alert and willing to work with whatever is present before us.

In the beginner's mind there are many possibilities, but in the expert's there are few. —Shunryu Suzuki

When we love and accept ourselves as we are, we engage in the vulnerable act of learning without the fear of looking foolish.
—Laurence G. Boldt

The more I learn, the more I realize I don't know.   —Albert Einstein

The trouble with most of us is that we know too much that ain't so.
                                                        —Mark Twain

Children are natural Zen masters; their world is brand new in each and every moment.   —John Bradshaw

There is Buddha for those who don't know what he is, really. There is no Buddha for those who know what he is, really.   —Zen saying

The first essential in writing about anything is that the writer should have no experience of the matter.   —Isadora Duncan

A good man is always a beginner.   —Marcus Aurelius

It takes a lot of experience for a girl to kiss like a beginner.
                                                        —Anonymous

You can learn new things at any time in your life if you're willing to be a beginner. If you actually learn to like being a beginner, the whole world opens up to you.   —Barbara Sher

1. Beginning dancer. Knows nothing.
2. Intermediate dancer. Knows everything. Too good to dance with beginners.
3. Hotshot dancer. Too good to dance with anyone.
4. Advanced dancer. Dances everything. Especially with beginners.

—Anonymous

Meditation in Zen means keeping don't-know mind when bowing, chanting and sitting Zen.   —Seung Sahn

Tango, Zen, Enlightenment. . . Everyday life

Zen is not a religion, Enlightenment is not excitement, and Tango is nothing but Tango. They are just part of everyday life, nothing special. For example, since Tango is a walking dance, when we dance Tango, we just walk the way we walk everyday on the streets. As we meditate while dancing Tango, we realize many of our questions have been answered internally and become willing to face challenges ahead with confidence. We also realize it is time to get back to work.

Before enlightenment, I chopped wood and carried water; after enlightenment, I chopped wood and carried water. —Zen saying

Let's walk, with eyes looking forward, not to the floor! Because people in the street walk the way we have to walk in Tango, so we'll remember how we walk in the street! —Susana Miller

Zen open a man's eye to the greatest mystery as it is daily and hourly performed; it enlarges the heart to embrace eternity of time and infinity of space in its every palpitation; it makes us live in the world as if walking in the garden of Eden.   —D.T. Suzuki

And I feel that life should not be lost in Tango, but to regain Tango for life and at the same time do life more interesting.   —Susana Miller

And we should consider
Every day lost
On which
We have not danced
At least once
*   —Friedrich Wilhelm Nietzsche*

Tango is life on the dance floor. Life is Tango off the dance floor.
*   —Polly McBride*

Reality is where we are from moment to moment.   —Robert Linssen

Take the time to come home to yourself every day. —Robin Casarjean

Earth provides enough to satisfy every man's need, but not every man's greed. —Mahatma Gandhi

The best thing about the future is that it comes from only one day at a time. —Abraham Lincoln

The whole of science is nothing more than a refinement of everyday thinking. — Albert Einstein

Here are a number of exercises, which you can practice alone or with your partner to embark on your way toward meditating while dancing Tango.

THINGS TO REMEMBER DURING ALL THE EXERCISES:

It is important to be mindful while performing the exercises. To be mindful you need to keep in mind the following:

— Refrain from talking to yourself: that is, no self-chatter.

— Refrain from talking with your partner if practicing as a couple.

— Let feelings and thoughts pass by.

— Listen to yourself, feel sensations happening through your body, such as action and reaction, push and pull, friction, centric force, momentum, inertia, forward or back or turning moves. Listen to your heartbeat and partner's heartbeat.

0. WARM-UP EXCERCISES

The goal of this exercise is, as with any exercise, to relax your mind and body. Release energy by shaking your body. You can shake your hands and feet. Then if you'd like, you can lightly jump up and down.

1. INDIVIDUAL STANDING EXERCISES

The goals of these exercises are to establish good posture and recognize the importance of constant breathing.

1.1 Posture: The Right posture, The Right State of Mind

— Keep the spine straight and still, chin tucked in, top of head pushed towards the ceiling, diaphragm pushed town towards lower abdomen, and the whole body relaxed at the same time.

— Eyes may be open or closed. If eyes are open, look down about one yard away from you. Legs are spread as wide as your shoulders.

- Shoulders dropped.

- Knees straight but not hyper-extended.

- Weight is evenly distributed between both legs and on the sole of each foot.

1.2 Breathing: Right posture, Natural breathing

- Breathe naturally and evenly.

- Breathing air, which is energy for your mind and body, should expand *Dan Tien*, the center of energy below the navel, instead of chest. This is also known as diaphramatic breathing.

- Put your hands together and place them on the *Dan Tien*. Try to feel flow of energy while breathing. (Photo 1)

Photo 1. Standing with hands placed on Dan Tien

2. INDIVIDUAL STRETCH

EXERCISES

Through these exercises below you will learn how to establish and maintain balance in your body while moving. Focus will be on clear weight-shifting; make sure your weight is on one side of the body while moving.

2.1 Two-Hands Stretch up

— Slowly lift both arms until fingertips are pointed upward. While being lifted, the arms stay straight without locked elbows. (Photo 2)

Photo 2.
Lifting hands: beginning, middle, and end

- While lifting hands, shift your weight to one leg and pause and then notice your body. Make sure your whole body is balanced whether the body is moving or still.

- Lower your hands.

- Repeat the above steps.

2.2 One-Hand Stretch Up

- Slowly lift one hand until fingertips are pointed upward. While being lifted, the arm stays straight.

- While lifting one arm, shift your weight to the same side of the lifted hand and pause and then notice your body.

Photo 3. Lifting one hand, move one leg to side. . .

— Slowly move the free leg, to the side, forward and back. Make sure body is balanced whether the body is moving or still. (Photo 3)

— Lower your hand.

— Repeat the above steps with the other hand.

Photo 3.
. . . moving one leg to forward or back

2.3 Two-Hands Stretch Forward and Back

— Shift weight to toes while lifting hands towards back. (Photo 4)

— Shift weight to heels while lifting hands towards front.

— Make sure body is balanced whether body is moving or still.

— Repeat the above steps

Photo 4. Weight to toes with hands to back, weight to heels hands to front

3. INDIVIDUAL WALKING EXERCISES

You will experience mindful walking through these exercises.

3.1 *Normal Walk*

— Walk the way you walk everyday on the street while maintaining the posture as in Section 1:1.

— Observe one's own walking sequence and describe the sequence. (Photo 5)

   a. Start with weight evenly distributed on two feet.
   b. Shift weight to one foot.
   c. Lift and displace the free foot. Keep the lifted foot as close to the floor as possible without dragging or sliding.
   d. Upon placing the free foot, immediately transfer weight to the placed foot.

— Be aware of all sensations from moving body parts while walking.

— For each step taken, make a clear weight shift.

- Weight ONLY on one foot when moving, for balance and agility.

- Maintain same height while walking. No bouncing.

Photo 5. Srquence of walking

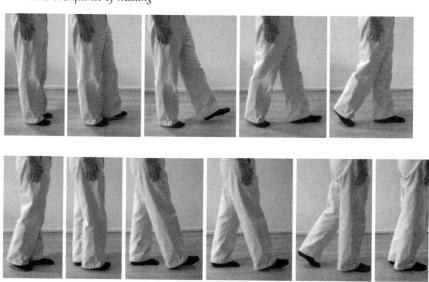

3.2 Normal Walk to music

Play a song and walk to the rhythm of the song. If possible, select songs with simple and consistent rhythm for this exercise.

3.3 Slow Walk

Walk as slow as possible. The body has to move forward or backward as slow as possible, constantly and continuously, while height stays the same and the body weight remains on one foot.

3.4 Slow Walk to music

Play a slow song and walk to the rhythm of the song. Alternatively, it is possible to play a song at a normal pace and walk to every other beat, actually slowing down by cutting the speed in half. Continue slowing down one's walking pace by cutting the speed in half.

4. COUPLE STANDING EXERCISES

Goal of these exercises is to help a couple establish a sense of connection between them.

4.1 Touch Hands

Both partners stretch hands forward and make contact with your parner's palms. Sense partner's presence through this contact of palms. (Photo 6) Try to sense partner's presence with eyes closed.

Photo 6. Couple with stretching hands to other's

4.2 Push Hands

From the Touch Hands exercise above, one person moves hands in a random circular fashion, and the other person's hands follow the movements, as if one person is the mirror reflection of theother.

4.3 Push Shoulder—push until partner starts moving

Both put hands on partner's shoulders and try to sense partner's presence. Then one person (pushing person) pushes shoulders of the other person (receiving person) until receiving person is forced to take a step to avoid falling. It is to be noted that

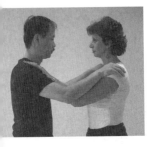

pushing must be accomplished by shifting one's weight forward, NOT by stretching arms, while the whole body remains straight. To accomplish this weight shifting with a straight body, pushing person needs to shift weight to toes. Conversely, receiving person must shift weight to heels, when pushed, to keep body straight before taking a step. (Photo 7)

Photo 7. Couple with hands on partner's shoulder

4.4 Repeat Push Shoulder exercise with different distances between partners.

4.5 Repeat above exercises with eyes or closed.

4.6 Repeat above exercises to music.

5. COUPLE WALKING EXERCISES

The goal of these exercises is to establish and maintain physical and emotional connection between partners while dancing.

The key idea of these exercises is to embrace and walk with your partner in unison. One person guides (or leads) and the other person responds (or follows). There are a number of ways to embrace your partner as shown below:

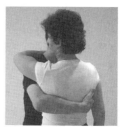

Photo 8. Follower's elbows on leader's chest and leader's arms around follower's lower back

Photo 9. Hugging posture

Photo 10. Embracing with one hand

Photo 11. Open embrace

Photo 12. Close embrace

As in Individual Walking Exercises, you can perform these Couple Walking Exercises to music. It is possible to slow down the walking pace by walking to every other beat, actually slowing down movement by cutting the speed in half. Continue slowing down the walking pace cutting the speed in half.

It is also possible to practice these exercises with one partner's eyes closed while the other's eyes are open.

Acknowledgments

With gratitude to the following artists:
Tomas Marczi (p. 2), Alan Ponze (pp. 6 & 12), HyoKeong Jang (pp. 16 & all the calligraphy works), Adriana Perez Gianny (p. 18), Peer Hirschbühl (pp.20, 24, 28, 32, 48, 60 & 64), Angelika Bardehle (pp. 36, 40, 44, 52 & 56), and Gene Park (pp. 69-73, 75 & 77-79). Also with appreciation for the dancers featured in photos.

More on Tango, Zen, and Tango Zen

For more information on Tango Zen including classes, workshops and private lessons, please contact Tango Zen House:
    Web site: http://www.TangoZen.com
    Email: TangoZen@hotmail.com

For further information on Tango consult:
    http://members.ping.at/kdf-wien/tango/
    http://totango.net/ttindex.html
    http://laue.ethz.ch/cm/htm/index.html

For further information on Zen consult:
    Zen Mind, Beginner's Mind, Shunryu Suzuki
    Zen Keys, Thich Nhat Hanh

About Chan Park

Chan Park is a writer with expertise in many fields including university training in science and engineering. He also has background in music, fine art, mind/body medicine, martial arts, and Oriental philosophy, all of which he has combined to create a unique yet traditionally related style of teaching and dancing Tango. His teaching and experience of Tango can be found at

http://www.TangoZen.com/bio.html.

He also plays bandoneon, a main instrument in Tango music.

With Eugenia, his wife and dance partner, Chan travels around the world to teach Tango. They reside in Silver Spring, Maryland, with children, Gene and Euni, and their dog, Licker.